GOD'S FAMILY
AND
THE END
OF THE WORLD

GARY L. HORNOCK

ISBN: 978-1-965679-39-5 (sc)
ISBN: 978-1-965679-40-1 (e)

Rev. date: 10/15/2024

CONTENTS

1

OUR FAMILY AND FRIENDS

The first book I wrote received an imprimatur from the Archdiocese of New Orleans to be advertised in its newspaper, *Clarion Herald*. I tried to bring the message about my first book to the Sunshine state. The eight-diocese (Church district) state has a statewide publication called the *Florida Catholic*. This publication requires a three-quarter majority to receive the statewide imprimatur.

Five dioceses approved it. The remaining three didn't. I did not try to seek an imprimatur from the *FL Catholic* because of my near miss the first time. The *Clarion Herald* staff informed me that the priest who approved the first book was unable to read/approve the second. The biographical information in my first books does not properly describe me. The ages listed in the first books are off by one or two years. To be the ancient dinosaur depicted, I would have been *held back* in school. If I was that old, I would be ready to "pasture-ize." The schools I attended represented a very white, Protestant, homogenous, conservative, and somewhat intolerant place. My parent's answer of "say you are German" (most people living in that area at that time were of Germanic descent) did not work.

We have an English-sounding last name. I am probably about 50 percent Slovak and possibly about 12 percent Germanic. Other nationalities likely include Hungarian, Italian, and possibly English or Polish.

We spent most of the summer in suburban Miami, visiting and living with my great-aunt. All those warm sunshine gave our family members olive-coloring. My complexion was darker than most people's, and even in Miami, I was confused with being Hispanic but especially up north. My ethnicity and race were frequently questioned by bigots. I was too Catholic, independent thinking, tolerant, indifferent, casual, and ethnic-looking. Although I fit in fairly well with the class of 1975, this community was not a good match. I was too much of everything this community wasn't.

My wife and I have been to over one hundred places from Salem, Massachusetts, to Miami to Los Angeles and Orange County that were much better matches for us. (In the north of Phillipsburg, New Jersey, the winters are too cold!) We are freezing at 40 degrees Fahrenheit.

I was in the workforce for years until I returned to college. I tried several jobs, including hall monitor in a high school, office jobs, and several manufacturing jobs.

College was an improvement over high school. After a recent scandal involving this university, I think LSU or UD may have been a better choice. Academically, the college I attended was excellent, but its top administration was morally bankrupt.

I attended college for four years and completed an additional half year during layoffs at the job I had been working at a previous location.

During the summer break from my first four years, I worked at an amusement park selling Italian ice. I was offered a fourth-grade teaching position at Lake Forest South Elementary School. I turned down this permanent position for two reasons: my mother's failing health and the required PPST, which all Southern states required. I failed all three sections of the test on my first try. I passed all sections of the test on my second attempt.

My parents both died on Monday afternoons, five weeks apart. My father was dying of cancer, and my wife and I were by his bedside. He told the priest what he considered his failings. After giving my father an absolution, Father George left the room with tear-filled eyes. My mother later died from successive strokes. I wrote the first two books in attempt to fulfill my father's deathbed wish.

After eleven months of 2000 in southeast Pennsylvania, we decided to experience the northern Gulf Coast for ourselves. We complained that up north was too cold, too snowy; and other, lesser issues (like Goldilocks and the three bears).

From 2001 to March 2005, winters were snowless in southeast Louisiana. Life offered different challenges. Winters were a combination of warm and sunny days, rain and fog, thunderstorms, and nights cold enough to freeze shallow puddles. Seventy-degree days are as common as thirty-degree nights. One or several days of intense rains occurred throughout much of the year.

Houston, Texas, to Gainesville, Florida, is the stormiest, rainiest part of the United States. West of Houston and southeast of Gainesville, rainfall diminishes.

From Lumberton, North Carolina, southward, summers seemed endless. Simple tasks like yard work were not so simple. You were living in a natural sauna. Sweat, toil, and trouble were a day-by-day experience. Spring and fall could be enjoyable with mild days, beautiful skies, and sometimes—believe it or not, Ripley—low humidity.

We never took the time, other than walking Ashley, to experience the activities the area offered. All work, and no play made Jack (and Jill) boring.

Mass on Sunday or Saturday night was the highlight of the week. Hours were spent with Father Jose Ladra, Father Bougeois, Monsignor Rareshide, and numerous deacons provided us with what we needed. Walking our dog Ashley in Terrytown, Slidell, and along Lakeshore Drive in New Orleans cleared our minds.

Highlights of our year were going to Delaware and Maryland points up north.

Visiting the special people at Christ the King's Charismatic Prayer Group was another highlight. Carroll and Deanie, Diana, Martha and Walley, Marian, Edith, Melanie and her son and grandson, and others provided us with friendships we wanted and desired. They gave us insight to life's challenges.

These special people made us feel special. We felt like we were in God's presence at this service. Life's worries and cares were swept away in a few hours. These two or three visits per year were special events for us. When we sang with others "We Are Standing on Holy Ground," we meant it.

Members of this group knew who really was in charge. Pre- Katrina prayer meetings gave us and others everything we needed to keep going. Flooding fears, dodging hurricanes, tornado warnings, high crime, and unbelievable insurance rates are a part of life in southern Louisiana.

In March 2005, we returned up north. We were lucky to miss the horrors of late August and September.

I worked at a different facility than I did in November 2000 with different job responsibilities and more and sometimes unfair rules. My wife's job responsibilities were also different than they were in 2000.

Deep South summers became a memory. We later purchased a cottage in East Dover Hundred, Delaware, several blocks from the Delaware Bay from my aunt and uncle. Some of our desire to be back in the south was satisfied by surrounding ourselves with loblolly and longleaf pines, southern live oak, and two needle palms.

Needle palms and dwarf palmettos can be grown in Delaware, eastern Maryland, DC, and eastern Virginia. They are the only palms which can be grown successfully north of Lewes, Delaware. Friendships resumed to previous levels.

Scripture mentions protection from danger (Isa. 43:12; Luke 10:19; Rev. 1:18). God has kept us safe from humans and animals who could harm us.

In the late 1990s, we hiked the back trails of the Merritt Island National Wildlife Refuge in eastern Florida. We encountered several snakes, including a baby rattlesnake and an extremely long non- poisonous snake. We encountered several alligators in this refuge.

Alligators are normally docile, sluggish reptiles, but they can be agitated if cornered and move quickly when necessary. They can live in salt water for short periods of a time.

We later returned to Merritt Island with our friend Beau. We saw gators from a distance, no snakes, and lots of playful armadillos.

On a related note, anyone who claims there are no poisonous snakes in Delaware are uninformed. They are rare. Cottonmouths (water moccasins) can be found up to I-95. We saw a cottonmouth crossing a public road in the Ted Harvey Conservation Area, southeast of Dover. A person encountered a cottonmouth at Becks Pond in Glasgow, Delaware. Read about this encounter online. Go to Google and type "cottonmouth" and" Glasgow Delaware."

On October 15, 2002, we were walking in a "safe" suburban area among shady trees. We listened to one friend's poor advice, which resulted in our being out later than we originally planned. God provided us with another friend who tried to prevent, with several attempts, this incident.

A short black man jumped out of an older sedan, carrying a pistol. My petite wife (not *Animal Planet*'s "Pit Boss" petite) looked like an easy target. He did not see me immediately. She was playing tug-of- war with this armed man, who looked at me and said, "I don't want to hurt your woman. I just want her (obscenity) purse."

I said to her, "Just give him your (obscenity) purse."

He jumped back into the car, which quickly disappeared into the night.

The police were in a state of disbelief that this crime happened when/where it did.

Slums are not the only place where crimes occur. They can also happen in commercial suburban areas, where lighting can be obstructed by trees. Ladies, please do not carry a purse at night.

After Ashley died, we rescued a sheltie/cattle dog mix we named Ashlen. Ashlen had a short life with us, but her last years were her happiest.

God and Ashlen were with my wife many years later. On a warm sunny afternoon, they were approached by a man wearing a ski mask in southeast Pennsylvania suburbia. As they were walking, Ashlen sensed danger. The fur on her back was erect, and she displayed her pretty teeth. (Look, I don't need dentures!) She was about to go for his throat, and he turned and ran away.

After Hurricane Katrina, my eyes were sore from days of crying— the people, the pets, those suffering and dying without human dignity. Thousands died, and their earthly bodies were waiting to be identified and reclaimed by loved ones.

Questions for us remained. What about Lilly and her family? John and Florence? Pat and his family? What about all God's chosen people from CTK's prayer group: Carroll and Deanie, Diana, Martha, and Walley? Marian? Edith? Melanie, her son, and grandson? And other kind and caring individuals who made this supplement to the Mass real and alive?

A common saying in this group was "When I get to purgatory…"

Most of these special people did not need to worry about being purged for anything. Many had experienced so much penitential suffering that many/all of their venial sins have been removed (Num. 6:24–26).

Ashlen was succeeded by Cammy in 2009, another abused shelter dog, who was rescued from the same northeastern Maryland facility that Ashlen was adopted from. Although some people are afraid of her, our cattle dog mix was the most improved dog we had ever owned.

I admire Tia Torres and her family (*Animal Planet*'s "Pit Bulls & Parolees"), who recycle both dogs and people (Mark 9:41; Luke 10:33–37).

God has blessed me with a great family (my wife and several dogs). My extended family includes my brother, John, and his three grown children and his loving caregiver Ellen. He was severely afflicted with prostate cancer. After many prayers and aggressive, sometimes painful treatments, he later died of cancer.

Please pray for my brother and his family.

When we found out his cancer diagnosis, our family was as upset as we were by the death of our close friend Beau and the pain and suffering caused by Katrina.

I thank God for my family and extended family: John; Heather; Lindsey and his son, Jonathon; Ellen; and my in-laws.

I am not the easiest person to understand or to get along with. I bathe regularly, but my hair is not always perfect, and my casual mix-and-match attire ordinarily comes from Goodwill and other thrift stores.

My in-laws include my mother-in-law, father-in-law, sister-in-law, and her husband and two sons. My wife has countless relatives scattered across eastern Pennsylvania, the Harrisburg area of Pennsylvania, Delaware, Florida, and California. My relationship with my in-laws has slowly improved from a C to an A. I count them as an asset.

I have a good track record for selecting trustworthy long-term friends with two exceptions. One former friend found "Mr. Right." Mr. Right called us out of the blue and threatened us every way possible. He coerced this former friend and her daughters to sign a no contact order against us! The whole mess is just a bad memory. She later married and divorced him.

The other former friend, Doug, abandoned us at his wife's request several months later. His wife was much more polite and tactful. She claimed hearing about work only made him sad because he was unable to work. These friendships had been replaced many times by new solid friendships.

Beau was a true friend with tough choices to make. His abusive wife wanted him to give up his relationship with God and his friendship with us. He wasn't going to risk forfeiting his faith or close friendship with us for a wife who humiliated him on a daily basis. He chose what the scripture calls the "better portion" (Luke 10:38–42; John 11:146).

He was found dead in his mother's mobile home. His death was ruled as a suicide. It was no suicide. His two daughters knew Dad was a great guy with a loving heart. He was survived by an A-plus grade mother, loving sister and her family, and many friends.

There are two kinds of friends: true friends and fair-weather friends. True friends are there on the stormy days. Fair-weather friends have ten fingers and ten toes, but you can't count on them.

A few months after Beau died, another friend of ours died. He was distant from God because of sexual abuse caused by a priest. He refused to hear about God from someone much younger than himself and Catholic. Before he died, his Protestant neighbor talked to him about God, and he was receptive to it, and we believed he died in a state of spiritual grace. Good job, Josephine. Well done (Luke 10:38–42; John 11:1–46).

I was on the mend from open-heart surgery, which occurred on April 4, 2013, in a large eastern Pennsylvania hospital. They successfully repaired two bicuspids, one heart valve, and another valve, which starting to leak blood. Thank you for prayers and well wishes. They prescribed the drug Percocet for pain.

I had nightmares and daydreams: images of wet sand, dirt and clay, and dead animals.

Satan exploited my fears: flooding and animals dying. I asked to stop using this narcotic and to replace it with acetaminophen (eight- hour Tylenol).

I needed mental detoxification. The first day, I watched EWTN and the Philadelphia newscasts. The names Father Joseph Mary, Father Anthony Mary, Father Leonard Mary, Brother Paul Mary were mixed with other names: Glenn "Hurricane" Schwartz, Nefertiti Jáquez, Sheena Parveen, Vai Sikahema, Sue Serio, Adam Joseph, David Murphy, and Melissa Magee.

A few days later, I added the Disney Channel with its stars: Debby Ryan, Selena Gomez, Jake Short, G Hannelius, and Stan the Dog. Several days later, I was reintroduced to *Animal Planet* with "Pit Bulls & Parolees" with modern-day saints Tia Torres and her family, *Gator Boys*, and *Animal Cops: Houston*. I kept Comedy Central and Syfy programming to a bare minimum. Some Comedy Central and sci-fi programs are morally okay, and some of it are a moral disaster. Some Comedy Central and sci-fi programs contain profanity (not obscenity), and some Syfy movies contain graphic violence.

God has been supplying me with the ideas to write this book every night since the idea was placed in my mind at our new house in Delaware. I talked with the priest and deacon Sunday morning after Mass at this Pencader Hundred Delaware parish.

They came to the same conclusion: If God gave me these ideas, do what he wants me to do. Our cottage in East Dover Hundred was sold in 2012 a few months after we purchased a home in Pencader Hundred.

2

GOD'S FAMILY

Much of what we know about daily living can be found in sacred scripture including the parables. Jesus spoke of a rich king who gave his most trustworthy subject fifty coins; another, twenty; and the most foolish, ten.

One day, he requested his money. His most foolish servant came back with the ten coins, which he buried. The second servant brought an additional twenty coins with the twenty he was given. His most trustworthy came back with the original fifty coins and fifty more coins because of wise investing. The king gave the other ten coins to his subject with the one hundred coins.

Jesus used parables to make concepts, which seem difficult to understand clearly. The real fact is there is one god.

Jesus's parable is meant to illustrate a very difficult concept in the clearest way I can.

Imagine if God had a different kind of family, not His real family but an imaginary one. God in this imaginary family had a son of His direct bloodline, the Jews (Ezek. 11:16–20; Matt. 5:17–18). His daughter and her many descendants were adopted by the most holy and precious substance in the universe: the sacred blood of Christ himself. This mother was known as the mother church by some Christians. This feminine, seemingly ageless woman (the Roman Catholic Church), had three children of her own.

The first was also a female, who had three daughters of her own. Greek, Russian, and Coptic were daughters of the mother, the Orthodox Church. There is a sexless son who had never married or produced any offspring. This son was the Anglican/Episcopal Church. There is another son who was very masculine and had none of his mother's traits. He had many sons of his own and three daughters (Presbyterian, Lutheran, and United Church of Christ churches). There were two grandchildren. The granddaughter was the Jehovah's Witness church. This church's beliefs contained some solid Christian beliefs (Ps. 72:18). The grandson was the Mormon church. It was in no way similar to the mother church. This is the end of this analogy. That's all, folks.

Are you considering marriage?

To understand Judeo-Christian mindsets, you may need to read my first two books. Liberals of any religion only work well with other liberals. Inactive Christians only work well with other inactives. Catholic/Orthodox traditionals do not share a Protestant literal's views enough to get along on a daily basis. Anglicans blend well with most Judeo-Christians, but Protestant literals could be a problem.

Catholic/Orthodox literals can usually successfully marry Protestant literals. Catholics/Orthodox traditionals can often marry Protestant traditionals. A person of strong faith (literal/traditional) can rarely marry a person without faith. Men and women, without solid beliefs, can trick a believer into believing they can change. It is possible, but it rarely happens.

Non-Christian extremists are only suitable for someone of the same faith and mindset.

Can a group of people be compared to a breed of dog?

Pit bulls are often loving companions but one of the most feared breeds if abused. If you see a pit bull one hundred feet away, you can identify it as a pit bull. You cannot tell if the dog is gentle and loving or aggressive.

Muslims have a similar appearance on the outside. Some are gentle, nonaggressive souls; others are extremists, who are willing to kill innocent people in the service of their god, Allah.

Part of being a committed Christian or practicing Jew is social responsibility. We are to try to feed those who are hungry or homeless and to treat others with respect. Part of treating others respectfully is not judging others.

Do not judge others (Matt. 7:1–2; Luke 6:36–38; 1 Cor. 13:1–3) because sinners can be saved (Matt. 12:31–32; Eph. 5:13).

Although some are unaware, we need to vote our consciences. For Republicans, this is not as hard on moral issues. For Democrats, choices are more difficult.

Over the past twenty years, the Democratic Party lost many of its best people. Kathleen Blanco (D-LA) and John Breaux (D-LA) decided not to run again. Kathy Giffords (D-AZ) was severely wounded at a shooting at a shopping mall. Moderate US Senator Blanche Lincoln was voted out of office.

Some moderates (Bob Casey Jr. [Pennsylvania], Tom Carper [Delaware], and Mary Landrieu [Louisiana]) have been forced by the liberals/radicals to cave in at times.

In 2013, the liberals/radicals were running the party. Gay rights and abortion-on-demand were now part of the national platform.

Party great Bob Casey Sr. is deceased. Former governor Bob Casey Sr. (D-PA) wanted to speak on the moral faults of abortion-on- demand at the Democratic National Convention in 1992 (not 2012 but 1992).

Other Democratic greats are no longer in office (Blanco, Giffords, Breaux, and Lincoln).

Christians need to vote for the GOP candidate if the Democratic candidate is too liberal.

Most Christians know that abortion (Exod. 20:13) and gay marriage (Matt. 19:46) are wrong. When the curtain closes in the voting booth, vote your conscience.

3

THE END OF THE WORLD

On April 20, 1999, in Columbine, Colorado, armed students took control of the high school. Students were asked by these thugs, "Do you believe in God?" If one student said,

"Yes, but I'm a Jew," he/she would have been shot. If other students would say, "Yes, I am a Catholic or Protestant or Orthodox or Anglican," the result would be *pop*, *pop*, *pop*, and *pop*.

Muslim extremists view Christians and Jews as infidels and make no distinctions (Matt. 11:28; John 6:48–58; 1 Cor. 12:13; and 1 Cor. 13:6–13).

Y2K (the year 2000 with its anticipated technology meltdown) was supposed to cause everything to stop working causing widespread disruptions in everything because of existing technology would be unable to recognize the new year; obviously, the round-the-clock work by tech people averted the potential crisis.

The year 2012 was thought to start off the apocalypse. The year 2012 had come and gone as well. I did include some of those potential events to allow the reader to know what many of the most informed people were saying at the time with the following warning: We do not know the day nor the hour of our master's return (Matt. 24:3–51). If we attempt to get along with others, attend Mass or other services, dust off our Bibles, and vote our consciences, we do not need to worry about the end.

On September 11, 2001, Muslim extremists hijacked three planes. One crashed into the World Trade Center, killing many innocent people. Another crashed into the Pentagon in Virginia, and the third crashed into a deserted field in Pennsylvania.

A Muslim extremist, Osama bin Laden, claimed responsibility. His evil acts caused two wars: One was in Afghanistan, fighting his sympathizers called the Taliban; the other was in Iraq.

Faulty intelligence caused a rumor that Iraq's leader, Saddam Hussein, was hiding nuclear weapons. None were found.

Saddam wasn't a Muslim, and he respected the country's Christian minority. His spokesman was a Christian named Tariq Aziz. Aziz was executed with Saddam.

Muslims dominate Iraq today and kill or persecute Christians. Pope John Paul II died in April 2005. He was succeeded by Pope Benedict XVI. Pope Benedict retired in March 2013. The papal conclave chose a very Christian successor, a Franciscan who chose the title Pope Francis (not Peter II!). Some Protestant eschatologists had heard that our new pope would like to improve relations between Christians and Muslims. (This move may have been to minimize the persecution of Christians living in Muslim-dominated countries.) Some of these people would like to assign the title of *antipope* to Francis. Clearly, Francis is not the antipope, but who will be his successor?

Hurricane Katrina hit the Florida Keys in late August 2005. Her path was uncertain. Some people in southeast Louisiana and southern Mississippi loaded up their autos and trucks and headed inland or out of the projected storm path. Those without transportation or urgent needs stayed along with the looters.

Katrina came ashore at the mouth of the Mississippi. It turned almost due north toward Lake Borgne on the Louisiana and Mississippi border. This landfall helped New Orleans and dealt a devastating blow to the Mississippi coast.

Linkin Park's song "The Little Things Give You Away" addressed what happened next.

The US Army Corps of Engineers, in an attempt to save money, compromised the integrity of the levee system, which collapsed in several places, flooding New Orleans's lowest spots.

They also built the Mississippi River-Gulf Outlet Canal, which placed New Orleans's suburbs to the east at risk for serious flooding.

The lowest sections of these areas filled with putrid water. The innocent suffered, along with individuals who stayed to have their own personal shopping spree. They took television sets and other electronics (no electricity, *duh*), guns and ammo for a rainy day, and lots of alcohol—alcohol and guns, the Louisiana staples, but not a good combination.

Cases of water, tuna and other nonperishable foods, baby foods, and diapers remained on the shelves.

Gunshots were everywhere. Who was shooting whom?

Suburbanites dusted off their guns. People wanted to protect what they worked so hard: their families, homes, and personal belongings. Heat and humidity, alcohol, and stress started to take its toll.

People were wearing down and making mistakes including the police.

Bad decisions were more common than good ones. New Orleans Mayor Ray Nagin was in his high-rise hotel room, complaining about everything and everybody. Everything was everybody else's fault.

Months after Katrina, Nagin made his racist appeal to save his own political career. He requested that black residents return to make it "chocolate town" again.

Governor Kathleen Babineaux Blanco (D) fervently prayed to God for help while everyone else played the blame game.

Kathleen was criticized by Nagin for wanting to help suburbanites in need. The world was helping New Orleans.

In St. Bernard Parish (the patron saint of the lost and forgotten), people experienced most of what New Orleans did.

The Murphy Oil company had a major leak at its storage facility near Meraux. Petrochemicals poured into the standing water. All the major networks were guilty of racism because all the world was watching black residents committing crimes or being rescued. Governor Blanco contracted to have the roof of the Louisiana Superdome repaired, which saved this famous structure.

Oakwood Center Mall in suburban Terrytown was looted and set on fire on August 31, 2005. Over 75 percent of the stores were damaged. Other malls—Lake Forest Plaza, New Orleans Center, and suburban Belle Promenade—never reopened.

There was a DVD "Events of Hurricane Katrina and the Aftermath 2005" released by a genius volunteer firefighter Marty Lee Martin, which was by far the best and least racist documentation of the hurricane. Marty Lee Martin lived in Terrytown at the time and later moved to Montz in St. Charles Parish.

Christ the King RC Church in Terrytown was heavily damaged by storm force winds, and Father Jose Ladra was faced with many challenges. On a related note, the members of their prayer group and others we knew living in the area survived Katrina and experienced no flooding. Our Lady of Lourdes Church in Slidell was reduced to rubble.

Father Arthur Ginart died in his church in Lake Catherine as Katrina destroyed it. The good captain went down with his ship. Heaven needed a good chaplain to help those in need.

Many innocent thousands died during one of the worst disasters in our lifetime.

Southern Louisiana has always used the fleur-de-lis (the French cross) as its symbol. Southeast Louisiana has always marched to the beat of a different drummer. Large parties and parades, spicy cooking, and unique people are part of this gumbo.

New Orleans is the home of the nation's largest black Catholic population and the South's largest transgender population. The saints came marching in in large numbers from the northern Gulf Coast in 2005. Heaven and purgatory were more vibrant because of these unique, creative people who let the good times roll in spite of everything.

Barrack Obama was sworn into the presidency in 2009. He is not the Antichrist as some presume. The Antichrist appeared with answers to unsolvable problems. Obama was merely a spokesman who could sound like a rational moderate for union members, families, and the military. When he spoke to gays, lesbians, bisexuals, Planned Parenthood (an organization which performs abortions), or Muslims, he told them what they want to hear. He is a Christian, but he supported causes most committed Christians consider morally wrong.

The idea of a black president is not a bad one; just do not pick the first person who wants the job.

Mayor Michael Nutter (D-Phi), Herman Cain (R), Condoleezza Rice (R), or Supreme Court Justice Clarence Thomas are all far less radical than Obama.

There is no difference between Obama and Hillary Clinton. There are women who are far better for our country than Hillary, including former governor Kathleen Blanco (D-LA), Blanche Lincoln (D-AR), Gabby Giffords (D-AZ), and Condoleezza Rice (R).

The best of all Republicans is the moderate and morally conservative governor of New Jersey, Chris Christie. He is by far one of the best governors since Blanco left office. He makes governors O'Malley (D-MD), Markell (D-DE), and Corbett (R-PA) look pathetic in comparison.

In January 2010, Obama approved of repealing "don't ask, don't tell." It protected gay military personnel from harm. It was a good idea, which may have needed a little fine tuning to work as it was originally intended. If the information was requested, the information should be provided without fear of dismissal.

Gay soldiers, sailors, airmen, or marines should not be allowed to openly flaunt their sexuality in front of individuals who would harm them. If someone wants to be openly gay, there is always live theater or ABC (but not the Disney Channel).

A couple of months later, Obama approved of a bill with few good ideas to keep health costs manageable. It prevented low-income people from using hospital emergency rooms to receive basic care and provided basic medical care for everyone (a good idea if it isn't abused).

Liberals/radicals attempted to add provisions to this law. If someone is unable to work because of disability or is unable to find employment, he/she should be provided with basic care.

People with no desire to work should be forced to purchase basic health insurance at group rates. The employed should be forced to purchase the same as a minimum unless his/her spouse/partner carries insurance for his/her family.

Abortion and contraceptives should not be covered by national health care, and no public funds should be used for these purposes.

The 2010 Super Bowl was our family's favorite as well as the favorite of those precious people who lost so much during Katrina.

The Saints beat the Colts. Was this historic win God's way of telling residents of the northern Gulf Coast that better days were ahead? I hope so.

Sean Payton, Drew Brees, and all the others worked together as a team. "Who dat thinks they are going to beat them Saints? Who dat" (the New Orleans Saints chant).

The Deepwater Horizon oil rig exploded in the Gulf of Mexico on April 20, 2010, killing eleven people and injuring many more. There were 4.9 million barrels of oil seeped into the gulf. In July 2010, it was successfully capped.

Several Roman Catholic priests were accused, and some were found guilty, sexually abusing children.

The church should have stopped the abuse. A priest found guilty should have been kept away from children at all costs.

Reassigning abusers as prison or military chaplains or permanently assigning them to a diocesan desk job was the solution. Some lost their respect for the mother church because of the church's slow response. Pope Francis promised quick response to allegations on April 5, 2013.

Pennsylvania State University had its own sex scandal, involving a mentally ill pedophile named Jerry Sandusky. Jerry was unaware of the seriousness of his actions and should be permanently placed with the mentally ill. Joe Paterno (the head athletic coach at Pennsylvania State) and his assistants did their part to stop the abuse and should not be punished.

President Graham Spanier was aware of these sex acts and did nothing to stop it. Spanier and an unknown coconspirator tried to cover it all up.

One investigator was found dead under suspicious circumstances. Graham should be punished far more severely (Luke 12:47–48) than Jerry (Luke 12:48). Graham is morally culpable for all of the abuse (Spanier charged with concealing abuse at PSU (www.chronicle.com/../135510). Go, Les Miles and LSU! We are fans of the "Who Dats" and the "Bayou Bengals" from Baton Rouge (LSU).

Hurricane Sandy came ashore in October 2012. Like Katrina, Sandy caused massive destruction and misery. Staten Island, Long island, and the New Jersey shore from Atlantic City to Keansburg bore the brunt of the storm. God spared the Delaware and Maryland shore communities from Assateague to Augustine Beach, including Rehoboth Beach, Delaware.

Rehoboth Beach; Provincetown, Massachusetts; and Key West are the gayest beach towns on the East Coast. Hurricane Katrina hit a few days before the Southern Decadence festival. This gay Mardi Gras was probably tolerated by the public and encouraged by the business community to bring in money during the slow summer season. Rehoboth Beach's lawmakers were the prime sponsors of the Delaware Marriage Equality Act.

This morally bankrupt bill was signed into law by Governor Markell immediately. This law was to please the gay people in Rehoboth Beach and larger cities. Family-oriented towns like Kitts Hummock, Glasgow, and Bear are not going to benefit from this change. Gay people, in some rural areas, might place themselves in danger as a result of this change.

On December 14, 2012, a mentally ill son went into the elementary school his mother taught in Sandy Hook, Connecticut, and shot twenty children and six teachers. He later killed his mother and himself. The surviving students were reassigned to a school in neighboring Newtown.

The Boston Marathon race is a national treasure. On April 23, 2013, two Muslim brothers planted several bombs along its route. Three people died, and 264 were injured. This race rewarded the efforts of athletes who trained for months. Two brothers from the Muslim-dominated part of Southern Russia caused this tragedy. One died on the scene, and the other would be booked on federal charges.

At 3:45 p.m. on May 20, 2013, an F5 tornado hit Moore, Oklahoma, killing twenty-four people and injuring many more. It destroyed 13,000 homes in its seventeen-mile path.

An F5 tornado is the strongest type of tornado with winds exceeding two hundred miles per hour.

On May 23, 2013, 60 percent of the Boy Scouts National Committee voted in Texas to allow openly gay boys into the boy scouts. This change takes place in January 2014.

There is still a ban on openly gay men from becoming Boy Scout leaders. Now the gays can celebrate their victory and look forward to the day when gay men can be Boy Scout leaders and lesbian women can be Girl Scout leaders.

Liberals/radicals persuaded the IRS to remove the tax exempt status from the Boy Scouts unless this change was made (Matt. 18:5–7; Mark 9:42; Mark 10:13–17).

The world keeps spinning toward the apocalypse at differing speeds each year. At some point, God will say enough is enough. Are you heading toward Heaven, purgatory, or the fate which awaits those who reject God?

Christ will come again in glory to judge the living and the dead. The rapture of believers will happen in the blink of an eye at some point in the future. Because you are living in a state of mortal sin, do you want to experience the horrific last seven years which await unsaved humanity at some point in the future?

The rapture may not happen in your lifetime, but other events can. Every day people die quickly from heart attacks and strokes. You can be fatally hit by a distracted driver (talking on a cell phone or texting) or someone who had a few too many drinks or high on drugs.

Eternity is forever. You may be one of the lucky ones who can have one honest confession or turn to God on your deathbed. The time to receive penance (what Protestants call *repenting*) is now. Swallow your pride and allow whatever it is that you are ashamed to be forgiven once and for all. Like most priests, God has heard it all before.

Please join the twelve apostles, the Virgin Mary and Joseph, John the Baptist, and former governor Bob Casey Sr. (D-PA) in God's presence. Judas Iscariot is probably still being purged, but he is in the presence of Jesus and His Father (Matt. 12:31–32).

Pilate and Herod wanted to release Jesus, not crucify Him. Herod had John the Baptist beheaded at his daughter's urging (Luke 9:7–9; Matt. 14:1–12; Mark 6:14–29; Luke 3:3–20; John 1:6–37; John 3:24–26).

Do not join Annas and Caiaphas (Matt. 21:23–45, 53; John 15:23–25), terrorist Osama bin Laden, German killer of thousands of Jews and Poles Adolf Hitler, and Russian barbarian Joseph Stalin in eternal punishment in the fires of hell.

A final note: Please recite the Our Father (Lord's Prayer) and Lamb of God prayers daily. Pray for those you love for God to help them or heal them. God is always listening. Please recite the Nicene Creed or Apostles' Creed at least once a week. God is saying to you, "We need to talk."